THE
NEW
WORLD
ORDER

SANDY ROSS

'YARALDI' CONSCIOUSNESS NURTURING

Ordering Information:

Prime Seven Media
518 Landmann St.
Tomah City, WI 54660

Printed in the United States of America

CONTENTS

CHAPTER ONE

NEITHER BLACK NOR WHITE

Living down on country for 18 months, gave me insight to what was happening previously. Wurruwarrin was revisited, thank you to the Berndts, and Di Bell, the archeologists that gave me the proof for my two books to be gazetted into the South Australian Library

This opened for me recognition of **Wurrwarrin, Miwi-Soul Sacred Lore** and obtaining my Wurrwarrin PMA (Private Membership Association)

The articles covered in this review were at this time:

Integration of Mental Health, Suicide Prevention and Drug Alcohol Services-

1. Substance abuse intervention: Facilitating behavior change the key.
2. Bridging cultures; psychologists working with Aboriginal clients.

Littlefield, L. (2004) Integration of Mental Health, Suicide Prevention and Drug Alcohol Services- but how? *Inpsych: The Bulletin of the Australian Psychological Society*, **vol.?, no.?**, pp. 7-8.

Littlefield (2004) considers how the services regarding the influences of alcohol use and drug taking can be monitored together successfully. This is where my workshops agree with MindMatters (Mindframe Resources) in the article, because it is important that children can obtain valuable information regarding support, and learn ways to cope with their parents who were/are suffering from illnesses related to drug and/or mental health problems. I find the foundation of supply, demand and harm reduction involving the endorsement by the Ministerial Council of Drug Strategy also conducive to my workshops, which are abou**t networking and** benefiting sections of the community who have become isolated through physical or mental trauma. The article also supports the need for unity. <u>**Pre-Approved Paramedical Professionals and mainstream Medical Professionals**</u> Ford, S. (2003). Substance abuse intervention: *The Bulletin of the Australian Psychological Society,* vol. 25, no. 4, pp. 9-11.

Judgement is a common human trait, and many forms of drug addiction can be deemed as arduous and as Ford (2003) states, specialized treatment is needed. There needs to be genuine support in assisting individuals or groups to maintain motivation, and find a purpose that will encompass change. Many clients being treated are surrounded by stigma and do not feel that they have empathy from practitioners and/or counselors, who many say, as noted in this article, are focused on drug intervention. A number of clients are aware of this reaction and this helps to place a wall between client and practitioner.

In my workshops I maintain that people are the most important factor and introduce individual story telling, so that their pain and emotions can be listened to. Trauma can happen in every person's life, and I have found in workshops that everybody's perception of their trauma varies, but each is nonetheless important. As the article suggests, drugs are used as an initial solution to detract from the trauma, but if the problem is not looked at, and dealt with using other interventions, the drug solution will only get worse. At this stage of existence there was a need to treat prescribed and recreational drugs as a **major health crisis.** I believe it is important that empathy with the person and a trusting relationship becomes a priority in the relationship. In my workshops it is important to allow the client to change at their own pace (if they choose to do so) and this involves individual consultation as well as group sessions. There is a need to address this health and social issue, and to put into place strategies that can encourage a holistic approach to healing. As the article promotes, options and support are necessary because the effects are well known and it is time to move to the next stage. Diversion and prevention of drug use by youth has to be examined by not more education and control, but by understanding why there is a need to take them. Assertive skills can be learnt, so that individuals can manage peer group pressure, and this suggestion supports my plan to educate groups by offering a program for **Diverse Cultural Holistic Healing.**

Data from psychologists could be utilized to intervene and instill positive behavioral changes, thus bringing into focus ethical dilemmas, which have become a major concern for all parties. The therapeutic process means a non-judgmental attitude has to be taken, whilst also looking at assumptions and stigma which will play an important role in this prevailing therapeutic relationship. Trust is an important co-action and if the relationship has not been built on it, respect for each other's position will deteriorate.

Ford, S. (2003). Bridging cultures; psychologists working with Aboriginal clients.

Bridging cultures: Psychologists working with Original Peoples clients The bridging of Indigenous and Non-Indigenous culture currently – and as it has been done in the past, plays an integral part in my personal cultural background, and this is why I can agree with Ford (2003) and share her difficulty in grasping how the philosophy of Western psychology has little meaning to Indigenous and many multicultural societies. I also can compare and agree with her determination to obtain the highest education possible, because through knowledge comes benefits that can identify the resilience behaviors which are now prevalent in today's youth.

The big issue that has been noted in the bridging of the cultures is the vast difference between cultural interpretation and understanding. Because there are basically no guidelines, and no data established in this area of psychology, the professionalism and ethics concerning this subject need to be examined and put into perspective with the diverse cultures that currently live in Australia. It has been suggested by a qualitative study that since the mid-1980s many Western teachings did not have positive or worthy results for the (Ab)Original people, and I believe that was because of the mistrust and fear that encompassed these services, the traditional healers were still preferred. Mental health issues were deemed to be a way of separating families and dividing communities, so they were avoided. The way that an Indigenous person seeks support is to simply 'have a yarn' The clinical perception that Aboriginal people have of the counseling process is not conducive to their cultural background, and there is still a preference for a third party or elder to be involved in the relationship. The benefit of this procedure is that the trust and respect of family or community elders can have a positive effect on the person seeking guidance. I have also found in my workshops that the well-being of a Western person is treated separately, and by that I mean there are separate doctors for each ailment. The First Nation person has a holistic approach to healing which involves treating the mind, body, and cultural and spiritual matters as one.

Culture plays a big part in what Western people see as mental illness. The trauma suffered by loss of their country and places of habitation, and white society's spiritual ignorance of the "Dreaming" has had a long-term historical impact in that generations of Aboriginal people since 1788 have been depressed and dissociated from their land and spirit. The way that I can agree with Ford is to work with the knowledge that (Ab) Original people learn by preferring to be visual and to imitate, rather than Western culture which prefers to write down everything and isolate their emotions and feelings. The Indigenous person needs <u>the attention</u> to be focused on the situation, and approached at a narrative level. Ideals need to be respected also, if there is to be any success. It is important for all cultures to adhere to the traditions of dress, body language and other existing and important values. Only by recognizing this will we be able to learn from each other and break down the barriers.

We can't escape the true history, that is still traumatizing on a deep cellular level. This is important to know, as 'Get over it' needs personal interception for each story. People say 'I wasn't there, I didn't contribute to that treatment. **I** wanted t express my concern to the youth, about why the Miwi- Soul plays a huge part in their conscious awareness and healing. Proof that our bodies are 70% toxic, but can be released through the breath work. The Miwi depends on deep breath, and that is why I was able to get a mask exemption, from a doctor. With the mask, we are shallow breathing continuously toxic CO_2, leaving our respiratory and lung area vulnerable.

The relationship between the brain, nervous system and Endocrine system assists us in understanding how a persons's emotional state may effect hormone levels. The hormones are chemical messengers and bring balance to the body. Miwi cleansing uses all the facts to empower the brain and mind to heal, thus mind over matter.

This assignment, lead me to facilitate for the youth, just at the start of Covid 19. A learning lesson in itself. Fear was the ruler here, and it effected everyone.

A test of endurance, as change is not a known positive in the collective. Anyway, we went ahead, like ships in the night, with no rudder. When studying I chose 3 models.

Wurruwarrin Philosophy 507 08-Diploma in Community Development:

Module One: CHCLD514 B Analyse impacts of Sociological Health Factors on clients in Community Works and Services.

Module Two: CHCC506A Promote and Respond to workplace diversity with bullying, intimidation, manipulation, sexual harassment causing confusion and low self-esteem.

Module Three: CHCCD516B Government Structures to enable more efficient Sacred Community Development Outcomes.

The Covid 19 story, has many perceptions, but at the beginning there was real fear. I had my first group with 'InCompro Youth Group'. No expectations because the fear was noticeable.

To teach a group there needs to be 6-8 persons, so the interaction, and pairing off can contribute to body, mind and electromagnetic spiritual connection and exchange.

The maximum I had was three. This was the start of dealing with negative thoughts.

These thoughts depress our actions and deplete the immune system, sabotaging the Cellular Memory and Genetic DNA on a conscious level.

To keep positive, a youth who attended regularly was inspired, and offered his service to make these sessions into a documentary. Bullying was also happening to an 'Original Worker' which was interesting. What I had observed, was the programming since colonization of the negative behaviors had perpetrated into our 'Original Peoples' conscious minds. Astrology played a small part in my Ancient Alternate Education.

I used the example to form an active higher consciousness raising among the group. Chiron in Aries effected us all, from a collective level.

Feelings of Abandonment and Worthlessness. Listing areas where you feel worthy. Identifying the true values and how that serves you and others is a positive. The healing journey of the 'Wound' is a gradual process for healing, forgiveness, accepting and finally unconditionally loving the circumstances of your life that contributed to what you are today. We have to revisit the past to reflect, pause so as to move forward.

CHAPTER TWO

THE FROZEN ICE MELTS UNDER THE SUN LIGHT

This Ancient Land exists within and without an object.

This country is both a container of many worlds, within a boundary of mountains, desert, plains, rain forests, snow, hills, valleys and caves.

Without space, there would be no separation, and the entire universe would be one solid mass. There would be no growth in any form, and no evolution. There have been debates about evolution, so this to me involves our Consciousness.

This space allows us to know who we are within, which is our own personal religion. The polarity of space, which is exterior, is separate to the world around us.

The Miwi-Soul is the connection, or the bridge, between the physical and mental stages of Conscious Elevation. It involves the same infinite source, part of human characteristics, that guides us in this life time, and then the Trinity exists, which connects and makes a magical universe.

The Ice Age has proven, life appears, and disappears.

These cycles bring change, in many forms.

There needed to be from my own previous book biographies, a follow up, and a continual story told of the Nurturing of Australia's Consciousness Raising, on this most Ancient Land. They have prepared me to encounter how the Miwi-Soul, with its power taken from the past, and was represented in history as demeaning illusions between heaven and earth.

Through my journey and inquisitive nature, I found the answer to how humanity had missed the simple explanation of how it was the survival to a 'Oneness, Collective, Higher Conscious way of existence. To face all that comes our way, is to learn about the possibility to make change for the greater good.

The ice is starting to melt, with drastic changes not only to our islands in the Pacific, but also bringing many creatures of land and sea, facing extinction.

The boundaries were changing from the past, and the space was eroding.

Environment changes were also effects from a foreign system, that Traditional people had inherited from history and the World Wide Colonisation Take over.

A Lawful Notice Velvel Revolution Australia, presented to me, a personal case while I was advocating for a married couple, who had their two boys taken away by the Department of Child Protection. There were charges against the Matriarch on 10/12/2021. There was a Notice given which was the first attempt to make a statement with a word. The word was 'Genecide', involving Genetic DNA and Cellular Memory.

People of the Commonwealth Australia lawfully removed Corporation Ministers and their agents known as Commonwealth of Australia, registered in Washington DC. A foreign Corporation and under Section 44i of the Commonwealth of Australia Constitution Act 1900UK. None of these Corporate conglomerates can sit in our parliaments as a foreign entity, every minister sitting under those unlawful political parties have no lawful standing, and have been removed from our establishment.

This is were my journey started. I started making a checklist, preparing a document pack. Crime cited 'Genecide' and crimes against humanity and with, multiple breaches of Human Rights.

Wurruwarrin and the case against the Seven Sisters, written previously, in my book, Wurruwarrin Where the Wind Blows' and gazetted into the South Australian Library, stated multiple breaches of the Universal declaration on bioethics and human rights. The International Covenant on Civil NAD Political Rights, International covenant of Economic, Social and Cultural Rights, declaration of Helsinki, and the Nuremburg Code of 1947.

The Declaration of Geneva and breaches of the Constitution of Australia.

At the time of the Crimes Act in 1914, which gave any man or woman the authority to prevent crime, and also authority to use force, education and knowledge to prevent a person being arrested for escorting public services from property.

This is ironic, as our people weren't even considered or recognized in this Act.

Acknowledgement didn't come for 'Original Peoples' of this land until the referendum in 1967. So his means, that the convicts coming from England, and had the power, in the law at that time, to use authority and force, which is why the civil case was won.

The Letters Patent, issued under the Great Seal of Australia, by her Majesty Queen Elizabeth 11, Queen of United Kingdom and Northern Ireland, appointing a Governor General in Australia, had been issued incorrectly.

King William the 4th was given this tile for one sole purpose. He was Irish, so under the English Law, he was chosen to authorize the Letter of Patent, when South Australia was proclaimed a Province. There was arguing amongst the Commissioners on how where the 'Original Peoples 'of this land were to be dealt with that would appear to be a lawful situation. There was the issue that needed to be addressed, so that the Commissioners could organize a cover of what was happening before 1835, and which was still known as Terra Australis was happening from 1835, which was still named Terra Nullius.

Then in 1836 the decision was made for King William 4th to be given the responsibility of issuing this 'supposed' Treaty. The Irish, and the Scottish were exploited.

It would be recorded in history books that the Natives and Decendants could have the freedom to roam, without fear of retribution.

Mysteriously he died within 12months, so the English Commissioners, where then able to set up their inherent changes to this unlawful Government system.

The Official Lore Notice by Grandmother Lore is the Superior Lore on the aniuima (land). Information; TIBNLA Seed of Governance, China Road Acacia Larrakia NT 0822 Australia.

This was before 1835. Wurruwarrin meaning 'Knowing and Believing' and is the First recognized and gazetted Grandmother's Sacred Lore information in the South Australian Library. It was noted pre-Letter of Patents 1836.

Head of State was given to Allen Campbell, from Northern Territory, who won the case in 1983, Queen Versus Campbell.

The reason why the case was won by Allen (Oopy) Campbell, whom I stayed with at Pine Gap, and received valuable information was because of mine and his heritage, with connection to the Scottish Free Masons. Owen wrote to Geneva while I was there, to retrieve some valuable documents that went missing in Allen's case.

My PMA (Private Membership Association) Wurruwarrin PMA is a 'Philosophy' and a Political Contract under now Lore/Law via Private Agreements. This Philosophy is a Miwi-Soul Conscious Belief System. It is registered as a Faith Based Association (FBA.) This has been handed down from generation to generation, and involves a Spiritual aspect known for over 60,000 years on this Ancient Country. The Spiritual aspect of this philosophy was not acknowledged until 1943, when Maslows Theory found his work, and words to be challenged. The word 'spirituality' was not allowed, by the powers to be. Our inner psyche was not considered to be a fixed Generalised Collective Archetype.

The Wurruwarrin Ethos or Dreaming works with Vibrational Electromagnetic forces, and has now been proven and can be sanctioned. This then takes me to the court case in 1983 of A (Oopy) Campbell V Queen.

I made a visit to Alice Springs to visit. I was picked up, and stayed at Pine Gap, where a small community existed. My investigation and written gazetted book had already found the British Westminster system Court System, in ruling in the Chancery Division of the High Court of London on friday 25th june 2004.

The powers to be had been set up, regarding the Free Masons. The information obtained while speaking to Allen, regarding this issue, gave me the answer to why I had to fly to Alice Springs NT. regarding the this important story.

The Scottish, who over history have had their issues with England. They originally placed their building practices as an honorary profession, thus the Free Masons.

When the Colonisers from England arrived in N.S.W. the Freemasons gave an unofficial 'go ahead' to the Convicts and new Settlers that the 'Blacks' can be shot. The land will become used for Agriculture, and it will be available for ownership. They are only guardians, so have no legal rights.

In South Australia, Ngarrindjeri (NAC) Corporate Body means 'Belonging to MEN' and refers to tribal constellation. Unified Cultural Block under the church at Raukan (formaly Pt McLeay Mission. Irene Watson argued this cultural construct which was imposed on many tribes, to form this Ngarrindjeri group. www nntt. gov.au ALRA enables Aboriginal Land Councils claim Crown Land.

LALC (Land Aboriginal Land Councils) can have land transferred to them in freehold title, if at the time of the claim, the land is among other requirements.www.coorong.sa.gov.au

This is why I have been ignored, and my claim to have my name _under_ great grand-dads name George Makeri No 70 on the Native Title.

NTA now as an overview for future Acts in Section 227, and sets out that, if an act affects Native Title through mining tenement, building public infrastructure services or facilities and the compulsory acquisition of land, it will be invalid.

'Procedual Rights' through register NNTT's Register of ILUA's format will be challenged again. The South Australian Government Royal Commission in 1995 'TREASONED' our Moiety regarding the Discrimination Act regarding the Constitutional Law Section 51

Private Membership Corporations can't make Law.

My freedom Based Association, 'Wurruwarrin Sacred Lore' can challenge the Church. Other PMA are still based under the 'Public Human Herd' under Guardianship of the Barr. The Moiety Customary Lore, under Aunty Sandy Ross of Yaraldi Body Politics, is my Social Compact.

CHAPTER THREE

PRE-REQUISTE FOR ANCIENT LORE

An inborn activity that reflects the wisdom of Ancient Survival Techniques, uses Alternate Therapy that Deconstructs Traumatic Experiences through Implementing Narrative Work and using Symbols (Pearson & Wilson 2002)

<u>**FIRST:**</u> 'Wise Women of the Dreamtime Polarities'

Ancient Alchymia(17th century Science of Natural Substances) and Ngankari Dreaming Lore contains balance and harmony between opposing forces.

The Miwi-Soul connection, and does not change for centuries.

Since the beginning of time, it is handed down to those that believe, and are open to receiving. It's guiding force to re-imagining strengthens the natural world. The naval string Relationship, if not adhered to will cause disease. Anatomy of illness is an identity. Genetic identities are stored in the cellular memory, and stored until discovered, experienced and released. Positive energy charges are challenged by negative energy charges, which overtake.

A solution of balance needs to be addressed. My story on being enlightened, eliminated the identity of shame, and my truth was knowing and believing and identifying it as my Miwi-Soul.

This is part of the genetic coding or blueprint lying deep in the DNA. This information relates to diseases, and behavior patterns. These genes can carry socio-cultural information that can be transformed. Two-Way Culture presentation allows the negative of five modules, to be re-directed toward a positive outcome. It is important to look at these polarities that combine a physical, mental and a spiritual holistic approach.

- Irrational Beliefs (Western) Equality versus Equity (Alchymia)
- Panspiritism(Western) versus Just Being (Ngankari)
- Subjective (Western) versus Ogjective (Ngankari)
- Religous (east & west) versus Conscious Spiritualty (Ngankari)
- Shallow Breath (Western) versus Deep Breath (Ngankari)

The stars, were guidelines for Traditional People and Father Sky informed our people on travelling and trading routes on country.

The introduction of Astrology, Numbers and Enneagrame by Westerners, introduced science to embrace ways to manipulate humanity. This is one example by them of programming. Using numbers on a conscious level was a way to utilize the polarity of negative action, against a positive one.

I went back to my teachings, when I had my business, Body, Mind, Link Service, and refered to ' How the Numbers Relate to the body and Mind'

Number 6 relates to the Head, which was the focus for the higher-self development. The Pineal and Pituitary Glands are where the Crown and the 8th Sister has been recently Awoken, at Port Elliot S.A.

The Crown for 'original People' is the Spiritual Connection to Father Sky.

Interestingly, at this critical time, I was talking to a friend of mine, who is a Christian. The subject of the number 6 came up. There was a negative connotation from her, and I quietly asked the question?

Why is this prominent in your faith? Did Yeshua give a reason in the bible?

In Wurruwarrin's Birthing Process the number 6 is about knowledge and communication, and at this elevation it also involves the Pineal and Pituitary Glands. The aim for the 6, is always to have a goal and a purpose.

A sense of feeling inadequate, which leads to the negative emotion of _Trickery_ (negative). This is where the Freemasons actually found the number 6 could be utilized as their chosen number. They claimed it, and used the trinity of 666 to present as a demonic number, promoting it in movies, as a ritual.

The opposite emotion of number 6 is 'Loyalty' so I explained to my friend that _Loyalty(positive)_ could be either for good or evil.

SECOND; The Birthing Process

Feminist Epistemology a prototype of engaged practice. The fact that the Missions forbade the practices of Culture, which went underground for decades, and is only now being recreated. The Yaraldi voices from the past, must not be forgotten, because the truth was not being heard, and it was stated by Daisy Rankine, Maggie Jacobs, Doreen Kartinyeri, and others, that too much theory, from the Imperialist Women's Studies, was distancing from the protocol of Wurruwarrin, Knowing and Believing Grandmother's Sacred Lore.

The birthing process is a Spiritual Ritual for the women, which connects the young, (Wanai Stage) This age ranges from 12-15years and 27-30 years. The initiations of woman hood of the different ages, is important, as I was able to relate my Astrology and the stars with validation.

Saturn the sign of responsibility, has different effects, with the puberty stage, with Saturn opposite Saturn, developing their social skills.

The Saturn return is taking full responsibility as an adult. The' Yirrar' period from 30-50 years, in Traditional society, were not judged for any wrong doings, as this was known as a learning period.

The women here were the mid-wives. They attended the birthing process, with a ritual that connected the baby's head cupped in hands, with the head and the Pineal Gland protected, and blessed with connection to Mother Earth.

'Surrealism' is about Revolutionizing Human Experiences, thus the challenge now for revival of a Sacred Lore.

Looking at the facts now and being able to encompass the survival techniques of the past and the inter-personal connections at all stages of human development, makes us look at the polarities of fact v fiction, scientific v religion. Looking also of the confusion of stability versus stagnation.

The birthing process is Women's Business, was disrupted, by involving the movement from one culture to another. This involve a revolution for all concerned, with issues having to constantly be adjusted and revised.

Directing the faults from the past history into the future requires patience, creativity, compassion and imagination.

THIRD: *My Genetic 'Walk- About' Memory*

The realization of this nomad trait, has been embedded in me since birth. My mothers story, saw her world interrupted by the second world war. Feminists over history, have had to uphold a prototype of engaged practices, which made women world- wide take on Patriarch duties. My brother and I shifted around a lot, so that was the beginning of us adjusting or living a nomad life. I couldn't settle, so I adjusted to life, learnt by experience, loved and took chances, and now can say, most times had no fear.

This is a pre-requisite for acceptance into the Grandmother's Lore, the first Lore of the Land. I have travelled and worked in S.A, W.A, N.T, Qld (Elders Mystery School) I also am of No fixed Address, with 3 caravans in different areas, setting up Sustainable Communities which has suited my lifestyle.

My Genetic DNA, in so many ways, has given me the life experience, and wisdom to fulfill my commitment to my duties regarding the challenge of the Unlawful Corporations now involved in Government.

Fourth: Higher Lore/Law of Australia

Proof needed for this title, is in my first book,' Wurruwarrin Where the Wind Blows', and period before 1835.

My train of thought, for change, was 'People Power' This is now the 21st Century has brought debates about a 'Spiritual War', and with this is the polarity of war and peace.

We are a land of many cultures and diversities now, and have gained so much to share. Recognition of the first Lore of this land invokes peace and harmony. The patriarch days of war, still continuing on many continents, must stop.

A submission to Aboriginal Lands Parliamentary Standing Committee Governance Inquiry with terms of Inquiry by Grandmother Mulara, has opened more investigations regarding the Patriarch effect within the Northern Flinders Ranges. In 1946/47 Adnyamathanha Senior Lore men stopped the Wilyara Lore in order to halt their people being killed for practicing their spiritual rites and cultural lore.

My concerns have to know how words can be misused, and as with so many other areas, as explained previously, our meaning of custodians of the land, have been hijacked by a subtle shift to ownership, which enabled land rights and mining interests to be traded.

Respect now sees men and women, all separate, but also looked at as a human being. Holding professional skills in many areas, with new creative ways of adjusting to the Pluto transition into the sign Aquarius. Traditional SIMPLE strategies, that I have instilled in my Tendi Meetings, will see less format, less paperwork, less procedures that have repeated in many ways.

The' Rights of the Child' Australia Treaty Series 1991 Number 4 Dept of Woman's Moiety New York 20/11/1989. Entry information force for Australia 16/1/1991. Australian Treaty Series, got publishing Service ©

Canberra Commonwealth of Australia 1995

Renee and myself at the return of the 'Seven Sisters Dreaming' which was taken away by the 1995 Royal Commission. The' Japanangka Paradigm' made note (West 1998) that our Ontology treasures Mother Earth beyond human life itself.

Marie and I came across the Eighth Stone, nearest the coast at Pt Elliot, and instinctively knew it was the Eighth Sister

Fifth: Unification Process

Under a trinity I always work with, I was looking for unification on a new Lawful Government that included Natural, Sacred and Common Lore.

I was included, in **Crown Exectutive Orders**, which to me involved the whole trinity.

This was perfect, as it gave me respect to set a standard for other Senior Lore Matriarchs. Opening to an International Collective Conscious Alternative.

The first process was to challenge the Attorney General, Kyam Maher, with a Notice on the 1/2/2023 to truly and solemnly affirm, under Wurruwarrin Grandmother's Sacred Lore PMA, that his position has been proven to be fraudulent. I was not at liberty to report my PMA to a false Attorney General, as it involved a conflict of interest.

Murray George from Pakalira, under the pressure of the Premier of S.A. the Attorney General, had a photo taken with Murray George, and arrogantly with a red headband on also., This was absolutely insulting and degrading from a **Culture and personal point of view.** As an initiated Ngankari Woman, under training from Senior Loreman Murray George. In Adelaide at the time his wife had just came out of hospital with surgery on her right arm. The Miwi-Soul healing, turned the kangaroo around, something I had to envisage on a higher conscious level. That was all the information I got from the interpreter.

This gives me and my Body Politic, Wurruwarrin Sacred Lore, official clarity to accept and be invited to combine my Two Way Culture History into the current system, and to bring awareness and change into the fraudulent actions of this current unlawful system.

The acceptance to 'Peoples Alliance' for rule of LORE/LAW which has a Global Energy, and was established in 2021. Rule of Law/Lore. This has just begun and needs to be debated, so many serious issues can be presented, and dealt with in a Lawful Collective manner. There needs to be many areas debated, but many serious issues are coming forward in areas of Fines, Mental Health, Forced Injections, Trafficking of young Women, Child Exploitation., and many other offenses.

Successful Stories need to be told, so that hope keeps infiltrating to the International Collective. Two successful stories was with Semma Donna, regarding her daughter, Takara being given back to her mother. Grandmother Freeda also having her grandson returned from Department of Child Protection.

SIXTH: Inclusions and Exclusions

My past business was 'Body, Mind, Link Service' and I required an ABN. When I was on my designated path, I made an appointment to the Business section in Adelaide, and stated I had Wurruwarrin Grandmother's Sacred Lore PMA. I presented my paperwork, with an addition, that my PMA was a Faith Based Association.(FBA)

This entitled it to be tax Exempt, similar to the Christian Religion, and exclusion from other Government Corporations, like Police, Lawyers, Health Workers etc. There was no complaint, and I was happy there was no challenge. It also fell under International Law.

Another Inclusion was a Common Seal Stamp, that is an advantage for a 'Knowing and Believing' Belief System.

When I was working, I belonged to the ABO (Aboriginal Business Organisation), which was Australia Wide.

The Common Seal was presented on their flyer.

In the 70's when funding was given out. There was a pre-requiste, which proves the government protected themselves.

Karpinyeri Incorporated Association, meant we, the government will give you funding, but you will be incorporated, and we will have the final say.

Respect for the preparation of plans for economic Development and Social Justice and for implementation of Development Schemes, regarding where the money is distributed. The Association now makes sense, because it really means that it is under a government corporation.

This is the proof, so before 1835, our Karpinyeri mob, were focused on running workshops, and were independent, but still did not have the freedom they desired.

Other Acts I have included which is Municipality Act 1994. As I'm interested in Sustainable Communities, that can be a pivotal point for improvement with the introduction of the Kerala Act 1994, which was added to the Amendment Act 1992. Statement of objects and reasons (Act 20 1994) transition from Rural area to urban (or clockwise) reservation of Seals for schelduled Castes, Tribes and Women. A more unified human preparation toward acceptance of all community groups.

Changes within our Education on a higher spiritual level was needed.

Wurruwarrin Philosophy toward Conscious Raising-Nurturing

An Oath & Signature BY MEMBER...

NOTICE: REGARDING SOCIOLOGICAL ISSUES...........................

....

....

....

Confronting Dogma -page 100 Five positive emotions of Original Peoples individual and community values

- Emotional EQ Intuitive Whole Brain page 58 The clair........ sentience (Miwi)
- Physical page 74 positive eye sight versus negative food chemical misplacement.
- Ego and Victimisation page 93 Self actualisation perceptions-business v spiritual.
- Humanity page 48 War history repeating itself-man repeats. Cellular memory and genetic DNA blueprint damaged
- Evolution page 23 the silent war with words. Civilisation needs wars
- Sacredness page 108 the Sacredness of the Trinity of Original Peoples involved the whole which was and is rich in science incorporating physical, humanity and sacredness.
- Feminine Ethos: page 15 Matriarch moieties altered- demeaned woman's responsibilities. Changed synergy of knowledge and how rational thinking was interpreted causing deep emotional conflicts.
- Cellular Memory page 92 personal effect Wandjina visions and feelings. Releasing physical past cellular pain- sabotaging self-trusting own intuition- making space for listening.

Animals: Raising awareness, prevention and conselltation.

'Wurruwarrin Where the Wind Blows' is gazzetted in S.A Library

CHAPTER FOUR

DECEPTION IN DENIAL

Westminster Law has been made on false evidence. The Freemasons had many ancient tools to utilize enslavement of the people. The false perjury of Queen Elizabeth whose birthday was on third of April 1926. Aries personality with her chart utilized for strength, and seduction.

Her birthdays were celebrated in June, which is another perjury statement to the people. Gemini personality was programmed into her soul. King George v1 in my view, had a false abdication, as he showed no strength in character, and in many eyes, broke religious protocol. This part of history was planned, with the knowledge of Astrology tainting the truth, in many ways.

The sychronicity of her birth in 1926, and the death of my great Grandfather George Makeri who was burial on 8th August 1926, opened a Lion's Gate Portal.

On the 5th May 1927 when King George v1 and Queen Visited South Australia, they stayed at Wellington Lodge to change the Royal's Title Register, locked in the Government Department until this year 2024.

The Title was passed down to Laura Kartinyeri a worthy person whose father was Pullume, leader of Kartinyeri Clan, father of Nymbulda Ngunaitponi, an early leader who resisted the mission and conversion to Christianity. The Freemasons at that time knew that supposedly, history would see that this statement was a distraction, because the mission through Raukan, had already had a hold. The Miw-Soul Genetic DNA and Cellular Memory, survives internally for generation to generation. The truth now had been passed down, by way of spirit electromagnetic connection.

Mind/Physical Matter over Miwi-Soul

The Miwi is our soul connection, and does not change through the centuries. Since the beginning of time, it has been handed down, to those that believe, and are open to receiving. It's a guiding force to re-imagining strengths of the natural world. The naval string Relationship, if not adhered to will cause disease. Anatomy of illness is an identity. Genetic identities are stored in the cellular memory, and stored until discovered, experienced, and released. They are invisible because it's subconscious. When you release an emotion or belief symptom without identifying and eliminating the causal factor, the energy pattern will continue. The Miwi is part of the genetic coding or blueprint lying deep in my DNA.

'Matter' from the dictionary is substance of which 'thing' is made- a physical or bodily substance. Cause of the trouble?

Dr Bradley Nelson - The Body Code:

When there is discord between the head (Pineal and Pituitary Glands) and the Digestive System, there is discord with the Miwi-Soul.

The Enteric Nervous System is responsible for both secretion and motility and is basically considered a separate, stand-alone system that belongs solely to the digestive system.

Although it functions on its own, it may be modified by the sympathetic or parasympathetic nervous systems.

The disconnection between the physical body and the Miwi-Soul is misalignment of bones, lowered immunity, organ and gland malfunction.

The physical is the hardware, and is the walking, talking computer system and the spirit is the intelligence within.

The Pineal is located in the middle of the brain. And is part of the endocrine system and also the CNS. It produces melanin, a hormone that helps stabilize the circadian rhythm and facilitates proper sleep.

Fluoride and other metals can cause calcification, reducing the function.

The Pituitary Gland is located at the lower part of the front of the brain. It is part of the endocrine as well as the CNS. It secretes hormones that influence other glands, to control.

If the Pineal become calcified, the parts of growth, blood pressure, thyroid- gland function, metabolism, water & hydration regulation, water absorption by the kidneys, temperature regulation and sex-gland function in both sexes are effected, and detrimental to a healthy lifestyle.

The Gut or (Intuitive Senses) are regulated by the health of the two Glands, involved with the Endocrine system or CNS. When in power the Shape Shifting can occur. For example the Clever Man or Woman in Indigenous Cultures. The belly button in connection at birth is the Miwi-Soul and is lukewarm after death for 3 hours.

Behind is 'Pechoti' 72,000 veins connected to life for 9 months.
UNMET NEEDS:

Offensive energies During 3 year ministry of Jeshua acknowledged entities. 7 of his 37 healing miracles included the casting out of dark spirits in order to relieve people of their mental or physical illness.

Pharmaceutical care keeps drugging and suppressing the illness while prevention is better than cure. Topics and discussions are dismissed.

Disembodied Spirits and Unembodied Spirits are ghosts that are Earth Bound.

The addiction then weakens the Miwi-Soul and the Ileo- Sacral Area is embedded with pornography or sexual misopropriated thoughts.

A Saboteur is a strong negative energy is present to sabotage the recipient.

This is created by the subconscious mind. Expressions of negative feelings toward recipient can be self inflicted. This causes intense self abuse. Can cause physical discomfort and interfere with recovery.

Questions need to be asked. Do you know the location, is it a weapon or a wound? Know age of occurrence?. Do you have a saboteur, we can find and eliminate?

Ngankari Healing x3 length of governing meridian, while holding the intention with other hand.

Repeat if necessary, but take time for prayer to higher source, and forgiveness of self.

The energy is PRANA or Life Force. The Blueprint of the Body are the Carnal Pleasures which reflect our overall MIWI-SOUL Awareness & connection to our higher spiritual realm.

It was important at this time, with my Private Membership Association, as a Faith Based Association (FBA) and for my

Grandmother's Sacred Lore to be accepted, and integrated with Natural and Common Law.

The issues that were relevant from my book, were set up to help raise the Conscious level of responding with a more Holistic out look, for the changes that were rapidly happening in society.

The Courts must accept and respect my Faith Based Association (FBA)

The Lore from Creator God Biame is our Crown, and resonates with Grandmother's Birthing Process.

This had been activated at Port Elliot, South Australia.

The Awakening of the Eighth Sister activated the Higher Conscious Awareness to our 5th Dimension and above.

This ritual validated the crown at the top of the head and replaced the foreign law.

This was a capital crime against a living Culture on this Ancient Land. There was a response within 7 days, with legality regarding the Children's Court of W.A Act 1988. Section 19B4 and is amended by deleting the crown.

Please provide a legal response regarding the ambiguity in relation to the Crown within the state of W.A. and with what right in regards to your Domestic Law. There was also a request to supply the Social Compact Agreement that grants your department board members the right to govern an estate or trust and collect a debt due to the Crown.

CHAPTER FIVE

THE MIWI AND PANSPIRITISM - CHANGING THE GUARD

Humans as we are mostly feeling a lack of 'Being'. The process of corruption begins with our own identification with this fact. My journey showed confusion with my different 'identities' which ultimately showed the negative emotions of vanity and emptiness. I had to finally be open to evolving to a 'being' of oneness within a more peaceful environment psychologically and physiologically. Learning how to leave behind the illusions of belief in a permanent outcome of thing, there arose a clear light of freedom, relaxation and truth.

When truth is missing through the ages, persecution leaves its mark. When relaxation is missing, there can be too much compromising and hypocrisy.

When freedom is missing there is claustrophobic entrapment and shallow responses, causing patterns of Cause and Effect.

There is a need for these to be observed when being conscious.

Sickness, suffering and death can be remedied only through transformation of our own actions, attitudes and ways of life. It's all found 'within'. Being conscious is escaping from the past negative actions of blame, guilt and shame.

It depends on 'Change of Thought' and intent for peace, goodwill and love toward Humanity. This is consciousness toward an authentic path. The choice is using individual consequences, using intelligence, imagination and harmony with the Self.

Aunty Rosie (Rosetta Rigney) stayed beyond the reach of the missionaries.

Mulparini meant 'Black Heathen' by the Christians. Miwi was alien territory, endangered under the heading of sorcery. It was rarely spoken, and with little reverence (held in great regard). This caused our people to become restless spirits and ill on a physical and mental level.

Aunty Rosie died in Glenside Mental Institution, same as George Makeri.

The Naval String Relation (Tindale 1930-52: 113) as previously explained through the birthing process, but also explaining Berndt (1993-245_ that it is part of our psychic life, a way of knowing central components of an Epistemology that relies on numerous oral traditions of elders, as the authorative texts within which to interpret signs and feelings. The stories provide the framework for understanding the signs. The orator provides a concluding section to his or her story, that brings the story home and grounds it in experience of those listening. The stories become what is happening now, not just in the past events. We speak of the wisdom of knowing the past, as a way of living in the present, and a way of ensuring the future. Our people communicate with the Ngatji (totem), the symbol, so that Ancestors can communicate with the living.

The extinction of many of our animals is taking away these cellular memories involving the past. This prepares us for ensuring new methods will appear in Nature, to guide us into the unknown.

Changing the Guard related to Yaraldi's Moiety Matrileanich.

From the Royal Titles Register on 5/5/1926, which was passed to Laura Kartinyeri, as explained, to cover the guilt of deflamation of Culture Royalty, by the church.

But then to Wilhemena?, Ethel Wympie Watson, who inherited the title from her aunt, Queenie Catherine Gibson accompanying ceremonies. From Mothers to eldest daughter, through sisters and then to oldest daughter of that sibling set.

At that time Dua-Yiridya division been spreading in Arnhem which was traditionally Matrileaneal, same moiety as the mother.

Since Colonization the Paternity Ethos has changed our Epistemology.

The Constitution of Laws of State are the basis of the Public Tranquility, the firmest support of political authority and security for the liberty of the itizens.

But the Constitution is a vain phantom and laws are useless, if they aren't religiously observed.

The inherent inclusion of Wurruwarrin Private Membership Conscious Association, with equal Tax Exempt rights as other religious groups, opens Human Rights interventions. To attach the Constitution of a State (which doesn't include Australia) is to violate laws, and is a Capital Crime, against society. If those guilty of it are invested with authority, they add to this crime a perfididious abuse of power in which they are intrusted.

CHAPTER SIX

CASH THE KING VERSUS DIGITAL ID

The days of the piggy bank saving is slowly slipping away. Progress is a word that can be misunderstood, and has positive and negative connotations. It actually depends on the situation that each person finds themselves in.

My interpretation of growing up with cash, gave me freedom. Ok !!!! people got robbed but the persons often got caught. Now we have to prepare for the technical superiors running a system that the average citizen has no idea, what is happening to the cash, they believe they have.

The onslaught of the technical AI surveillance state is an ID I do not want. I really have a freedom personality, and any form of real constriction will see me rebelling. It would be like being in jail, also movement, finger prints, palm prints iris scans, DNA, face scans etc, into a nationwide database, tells me to ask the question, what are we being protected against????

Is humanity at the lowest ebb of existence, and why is it that it does not recognize and appreciate its natural state.

Has the imagination, in its natural state been taken over by confusion, stagnate thoughts, boredom, and no-brain power?

Why do we need to give our verification and identification away, as I find that it is a sad state of affairs, that people who need this power and control, must be missing much from their life.

The Biometric digital ID, will enable the officials to have digital tyranny, and that to me, that is the sole purpose, of the supposed New World Order.

These steps utilizing new techniques benefit the Old World Order, working with the Patriarch Egos for a new type of 'War on Humanity'. It is a covert behavior, and they don't need guns. The new weapons overtly seen, with the power much more destructive.

Instantaneously identifiable, everywhere, no secrets, because of their arrogance, collocated and tracked, no sneaking around, but all your personal data collected and analyzed. Every aspect of our lives, health, finances will be openly scrutinized by endless AI profiling.

The history of this process was originally formulated and exported from Davos, Switzerland, and I always wondered when growing up, why all countries during the war, could bank in Switzerland, a neutral country.

What countries decided this? It apparently formed the key to the World Economic Forum, which later became the World Bank.

Can this be another revolution, to obtain assets,? Fifteen minute cities being designed, mass buildings are appearing, which tends to lean me toward a major lock-down, and people trapped in tiny apartments.

It is essential to protest. And to cultivate and harvest data on all citizens who are constantly blanketed by militarized 5G surveillance. Those who are forced to partake in Klauss Schwabs's transhumanised visions of teachings, are already being taught at schools.

At Wirritjin Proclamation at Alice Springs, saw Senior Lore Woman **Nellie Paterson** make an important statement, that was presented;

Our Creator Dreaming Ancestral Ngurunderi is part of the New Dreaming. (Matriarch Nellie Paterson prediction Wirritjin (2022)

Intellectual Biomimicry allows people see the current new meanings of the 'CROWN' which includes a polarity of the meaning of the word.

Sixth year of the New Testament. End of the sun (male oriented) and Old Testament.

This verifies to me that the sun and golden children from old the testament, are the golden sun children Indigo, Chrystal and Rainbow children now here, to set new standards.

The Eighth Sister is shifting limited beliefs, so nurturing the current behaviors is of great importance. This will release a flood of Creativity, Insight and renewed Confidence.

A Notification of Ancient Wisdom on LOVE

Put away the book, the description, the tradition, the authority, and take the journey of Self Discovery. LOVE- don't get caught in opinions and ideas about what love is, or should be.

When you love, everything will come right. Love has its own action, Love and you will know the blessings of it. Keep away from the authority who tells you what love is and what it is not. No authority can't tell the person who knows.

LOVE and there is Understanding

Jiddu Krishnamurthy (1895-1986) Indian Philosopher